Chloe Kim

by Grace Hansen

Abdo
OLYMPIC BIOGRAPHIES
Kids

Abdo Kids Jumbo is an Imprint of Abdo Kids
abdopublishing.com

abdopublishing.com

Published by Abdo Kids, a division of ABDO, P.O. Box 398166, Minneapolis, Minnesota 55439.
Copyright © 2019 by Abdo Consulting Group, Inc. International copyrights reserved in all countries.
No part of this book may be reproduced in any form without written permission from the publisher.
Abdo Kids Jumbo™ is a trademark and logo of Abdo Kids.

052018

092018

THIS BOOK CONTAINS RECYCLED MATERIALS

Photo Credits: Alamy, AP Images, Getty Images, iStock, Shutterstock

Production Contributors: Teddy Borth, Jennie Forsberg, Grace Hansen

Design Contributors: Dorothy Toth, Laura Mitchell

Library of Congress Control Number: 2018936107

Publisher's Cataloging in Publication Data

Names: Hansen, Grace, author.

Title: Chloe Kim / by Grace Hansen.

Description: Minneapolis, Minnesota : Abdo Kids, 2019 | Series: Olympic
  biographies set 2 | Includes glossary, index and online resources (page 24).

Identifiers: ISBN 9781532181436 (lib. bdg.) | ISBN 9781532181535 (ebook) |
  ISBN 9781532181580 (Read-to-me ebook)

Subjects: LCSH: Kim, Chloe, 2000---Juvenile literature. | Olympic athletes--Juvenile literature. |
Winter Olympics--Juvenile literature. | Women snowboarders--Juvenile literature.

Classification: DDC 796.93092 [B]--dc23

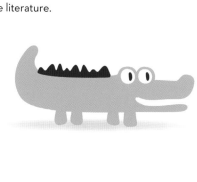

Table of Contents

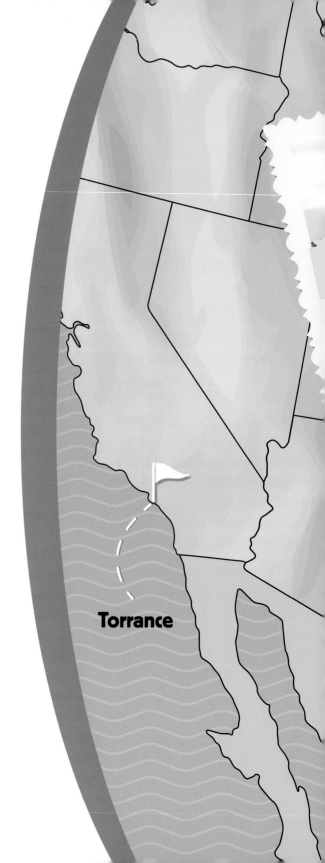

Early Years

Chloe Kim was born on
April 3, 2000. She grew
up in Torrance, California.

4

Being from Southern California did not stop Chloe from finding snow. She tried snowboarding for the first time when she was 4 years old.

X Games

Chloe had her first **sponsor** by the age of 11. She competed in her first X Games at 13. She got second place in the **halfpipe**!

WINTER ❌ GAMES

SUPERPIPE

❌ ASPEN

WOMEN'S
SNOWBOARD SUPERPIPE

1	CLARK	95.00
2	KIM	94.33
3	FARRINGTON	94.00
4	GOLD	91.00
5	CASTELLET	90.00
6	BLEILER	82.33
7	RODRIGUEZ	73.66
8	HIGHT	35.00

FINAL
RUN 3 OF 3

CHLOE KIM USA

BEST RUN 94.33 | 94.33 | ...NTLY 2...

9

The next year, Chloe won her first X Games. At 14, she was the youngest winner ever.

Perfect 100

In 2016, Chloe did something few boarders had done before. She was competing at the US Snowboarding Grand Prix. In her run, she landed back-to-back 1080s. She scored a perfect 100!

12

13

Olympian

In December 2017, Chloe
qualified for the Olympics.
Attending her first Olympics
in South Korea was special.
Her parents were born there!

Chloe was ready for her

halfpipe event. On her

first run, she scored 93.75.

Nobody scored better.

Her final run was a **victory lap**. But she was not going to make it an easy one. Chloe nailed her two biggest tricks. She won gold with a score of 98.25!

Chloe is known for her big smile and even bigger jumps. Her fans can't wait to see what she will achieve in the years to come.

More Facts

- Chloe qualified for the Olympics in 2014. But she was only 13 years old. Athletes must be 15 to compete in the Olympics.

- Chloe is also a great skateboarder. Skateboarding helped her learn a lot of snowboarding tricks.

- Chloe can speak three languages: English, French, and Korean.

Glossary

halfpipe – an event where a snowboarder performs jumps and tricks on a snow-covered, U-shaped ramp.

sponsor – a person or organization that gives money, products, or services to an athlete.

1080 – three full rotations.

victory lap – a run in which a snowboarder has already locked up the win, so she can attempt any trick she wants.

Index

Abdo Kids
ONLINE
FREE! ONLINE MULTIMEDIA RESOURCES

Visit **abdokids.com** and use this code to access crafts, games, videos, and more!

Abdo Kids Code:
OCK1436